MW01029914

FIGUREHEAD

& *OTHER POEMS*

BOOKS BY JOHN HOLLANDER

Poetry
Figurehead and Other Poems   1999
Tesserae and Other Poems   1993
Selected Poetry   1993
Harp Lake   1988
In Time and Place   1986
Powers of Thirteen   1983
Blue Wine and Other Poems   1979
Spectral Emanations: New and Selected Poems   1978
Reflections on Espionage   1976
Tales Told of the Fathers   1975
The Head of the Bed   1974
Town and Country Matters   1972
The Night Mirror   1971
Types of Shape   1969
Visions from the Ramble   1965
Movie-Going   1962
A Crackling of Thorns   1958

Criticism
The Poetry of Everyday Life   1998
The Work of Poetry   1997
The Gazer's Spirit   1995
Melodious Guile   1988
    Fictive Pattern in Poetic Language
Rhyme's Reason   1981
    A Guide to English Verse
The Figure of Echo   1981
    A Mode of Allusion in Milton and After
Vision and Resonance   1975
    Two Senses of Poetic Form
The Untuning of the Sky   1961
    Ideas of Music in English Poetry 1500–1700

For Children
The Immense Parade on Supererogation Day
    and What Happened to It   1972
The Quest of the Gole   1966

FIGUREHEAD

& *OTHER POEMS*

BY JOHN HOLLANDER

Alfred A. Knopf   New York 1999

ACKNOWLEDGMENTS

Thanks to the editors of the following magazines in which some of the poems in this book first appeared:

DISSENT: *The Parade*
MICHIGAN QUARTERLY REVIEW: *Then All Smiles Stopped*
THE NEW REPUBLIC: *Las Hilanderas; Dickcissel; A Shadow of a Great Rock in a Weary Land; Figurehead; An Old Image; What the Lovers in the Old Songs Thought*
THE NEW YORKER: *So Red; There or Then; Beach Whispers*
PARIS REVIEW: *Variations on a Table-Top*
PARTISAN REVIEW: *Across the Board*
POETRY: *Arachne's Story; Forget How to Remember How to Forget; Two Predators; Fire!; Digital; Afterword*
POETRY REVIEW (U.K.): *X's Syndrome*
PRINCETON LIBRARY BULLETIN: *Fancying Things Up*
RARITAN: *Early Birds*
SLATE: *Getting from Here to There (Part I); Where Was When*
SOUTHWEST REVIEW: *Getting from Here to There (Parts II and III); Long After*
THE YALE REVIEW: *Owl; M and M's*
WORD & IMAGE, Taylor & Francis, Ltd.: *Emblem*

Private Parts was first published in Lignes/Lines UCLA and The Armand Hammer Museum

Sun in an Empty Room appeared in *Edward Hopper and the American Imagination,* published by the Whitney Museum of American Art and W.W. Norton & Co.

Erasing a Bad Name appeared in Braille in *Lighthouse Poems,* published by Thornwillow Press, 1999.

Charles Sheeler's The Artist Looks at Nature was first published in *Transforming Vision: Writers on Art,* published by The Art Institute of Chicago and Little, Brown and Co. 1994

Library of Congress Cataloging-in-Publication Data

Hollander, John.
    Figurehead & other poems / by John Hollander.
      p. cm.
    ISBN 0-375-40484-8 (alk. paper).
    I.Title.
PS3515.03485F54   1999
811'.54—dc21   98-14208
                                     CIP

CONTENTS

FIGUREHEAD

& OTHER POEMS

For Judith and Michael

SO RED

Blossoms in the late
October light, of such a
saturated red:

what can flower now?
only the now awakened
dark and dull maroon—

like the unburnished
metal of copper beeches
shadowing itself—

of midsummer and
spring burning the japanese
maple's dying leaves

have fired the bursting
into astonished color
of the very self

of lateness, lastness
which itself can never last
longer than the few

moments—in this case
October days—it takes to make
itself intense in,

to put forth something
of light that had either been
waiting all along

to reveal itself
or more likely, escaping
its dead body of

leaf. It hits the road
with a visual halloo
as of a bright scarf

or a letting of
arterial blood in a
high ceremony—

annual, but so
loud this year—of impatience
and acknowledgement.

A FRAGMENT TWICE REPAIRED

Sappho, Fragment (Edmonds #43)

. . . Then I replied to them, the delightful women,
"How you will remember till you are old, our
Life together there in the splendid time of
        Youth, for we did so

Many pure and beautiful things together
Then, and now that you are all departing
Amorous passion gathers up my heart and
        Wrings it with anguish."

(Here the scrap of ragged papyrus gets to
Speak her piece, who, bearing textual witness
Down through all the violent aeons ever
        Sought restitution,

Sought to break the medium's silence, she who
Kept it while her fabric was rent and Chronos
Gathered up her heart and wrung it but not "with
        Anguish" or sorrow:)

"Sappho made me, Edmonds (J.M.) undid me
Now J.H., belated, restores the losses
Wrought on me by whatever at Oxyrhynchus
        Shredded me down to

Fifteen words, and a classicist's dusty guesses.
Hear me now who, virginal, carried down through
Many long and shifting but yet untiring
        Eras of eros—

Whether it were there in the splendid time of
Youth or all the afterwards I endured in—
Love's wild words, and those of jealousy standing
*   Just at her shoulder,*

Bore her character as my own and wore the
Impress of her singing hand in the darkness.
Cursed be those who patch me together but who
*   Heed not the gleaming."*

WHERE WAS WHEN

Unparadised, out of place
In all that is the case
(Envy, plotting, disgrace,

Fault, sin, naughtiness, crime)
We were thrown into time,
Being's new paradigm:

And thrust amidst that plain
Unwelcoming terrain
No life could remain

Unwounded, as the round
World's long tale unwound
The cord by which we're bound.

Abel the shepherd swain
And the dark farmer, Cain
Bring us around again

To death seen in its first
Form on earth: murder, worst
Crime, wherewith death is cursed.

The mark of being unjust
Falling on each death must
Infect the ultimate dust:

Here it was farmer killed
Herder on soil he'd tilled,
Founding a bloody guild

The farmhands of our foe.
The harvester whose slow
Cut lays the tall grain low:

Time, with his chronic scythe
Beneath whose swish we writhe
Whose repetitions tithe

Tidily, sans surcease
The time of our short lease,
Our little space of peace.

LAS HILANDERAS

Velazquez' spinners, at work in a large room;
behind them, and elevated somewhat, another
chamber in which Athena sternly regards
Arachne before the tapestry of the rape of
Europa that great weaver has completed.

Busy busy busy: they toil and also do
    They spin and to what final cause is made
Splendidly clear in the room behind—and, after all,
    Above—them: the tapestry is what the thread
Was for, the wonder of substantial image is what
    The tapestry was for, and as for the wonder,
It serves itself—crowning the end of what has tied
    Know-how to craft and after that to high
Art. And, above all that, as in an afterthought,
    The unacknowledging eye of an oriel
Window's blank stare, yielding nothing. The spinners,
    Their busy hands, the ladder leaning against
A wall behind them: all these point unwittingly
    To the back room of meaning, central—yes—
But from the great workplace seeming ancillary,
    An annex to the very here and now
Where what is spun is skeined without contentiousness.
    All that the tale of rival weavers might
Be told, and even told of them, the innocent spinners.
    Athena, and Arachne who became
A spider in her pride.

        You who would spin a yarn
    Like Ovid's of what you see and what you've heard of,
Consider Philomel and Arachne at their looms:
    One frames her images from desperate
Necessities of pain and out of outraged justice,
    One from the hurt of unacknowledged skill.
One depicts one rape, by mortal king of mortal
    Girl, the other figures many, of mortal

Women and boys by gods; one weaving testimony,
    A fabric of fact and pure, unthinking self,
One plying her shuttle with what she deems to be
    More than Olympian skill, filling with vivid
Wonder the texture of the very stuff of fiction
    She herself was made of, illustrating
Ovid's stories—her overwhelming immortal opponent
    Fashioning rather emblems of her own
Authority. She would not have it that the tales
    Told of the mortal lusts of the likes of her
Were truer and were done with better art than all
    Her mighty aegis-rattling. But she triumphed.
Arachne hanged herself by the warped fibres she wove
    Against, and thereby strangled her own cry—
Even as Philomel's ability to report
    Was ripped out of her mouth by him who raped
Her—the unfairly defeated weaver became the one
    Who spun the thread she evermore would weave
Her iridescent but all unimaging web
    With, to catch what it can of life but all
Too literally. Yet, consider her, among
    The spinners and the toilers with us now:
The humming industrious bee, say, gathering from the world
    Of fact the honey of what there is; the spider
Spinning out of its own guts, not the "expression"
    Of pain and longing, of delight and hope,
But the more profoundly formed cord of whatever
    Is woven into the matter of representation
Depicting by its structure, rather than, like canvas,
    Allowing its blank ungazing surface to
Be carefully defaced with images applied
    By an external hand. For, after all,
Who can truly depict whatever *Ow!* or *Ai!*
    Actually refers to? show or tell it
In any other way than pointing in-and-outward
    With the short finger of shriek that scrapes along
The interwoven pains of torn flesh and bruised bone
    And burning floods of horror? All is hearsay
When it comes to that. And that the spider knows;

And keeps her unimaginable feelings to
Herself, and representing not parts of life
    But only her high art itself, traps even
The bee, let alone all the nations of the fly, with
    What she has woven of her ultimate thread.

ARACHNE'S STORY

The skill at weaving was itself a web
All right, but not one I was caught in—neither
That, nor my oh-so-celebrated pride in it
Led me to want to show her my stuff.
But rather to show her—

Well, weaving, admittedly, can be the best
Of work: onto the warp of unsignifying strength
Are woven the threads of imaging that
Do their unseen work of structure too,
But can depict even while they draw
The warp together: my images are thus
Truly in and of the fabric, texture itself becoming
Text rather than lying like painting
Lightly upon some canvas or some wall.

It was not to challenge her,
Like some idiot warrior going up against some
Other idiot warrior: say rather
That it was to hear the simultaneous song
Of two harmonious shuttles, nosing in
And out of their warp like dolphins out
Of their one blue and into another.

But they will say that what I so wonderfully wove
Was all those terrible unfunny rapes her father
Changed himself into those shapes—flame,
Gold, swan, bull and all—in order more amusingly
To carry out: he was at least a connoisseur
Of bestialities. And not to speak of Neptune,
Apollo and the rest of them with their dallying below stairs.

No, it was none of that: who needs
Yet more porn, and yet more subtleties
Of formal treatment—legs, arms, and affrighted

Lineaments rhyming with patterns compliant branches make, and
Glittering vague waves and high suggestive clouds?

And then the whole array of nasty vignettes bordered with
Flowers and ivy intertwined—*intertextos*—says
That liar, Ovid, as if I had been reading
Some old book of the floral! No, it was none of that:
Who needs yet more vegetative decoration
Reducing the restless gaze to the blankly satisfied stare?

No: it was she herself I would show, the weaver
Woven into my web, the face of terrifying wisdom
Beyond the knowledge of Apollo and the tricky lore
Of Hermes. And that is what went into my web,
What grew out of my dancing hands and singing
Eyes and seeing heart. Her face emerged from
My sky and my clouds—was it not then something
Of my face, as well? She paused in her own work
And gazed at mine;
And to the Goddess' gray eyes
That image of her seemed, for too long a moment,
To be even more real than she was herself.
Too long, but still
A moment: for then her thread of thought broke as
A sudden wind blew through the chamber
We were working in, and shook the veil
And set the face of wisdom a-trembling,
Which with trembling gaze she coldly noted.

And that was all for weaving and for me.

All the mechanics and the pain—oh oh the pain
Of the transformation will go undescribed.
No, there will be none of that.
Say only that here I am, what I have never
And yet somehow ever been.

Back then when I was not as I am,
Spinning my jail of gossamer,

But wove, in and out, the shuttle working
Almost at—should I say, its own sweet will?
Now I spin instead of weaving, and make
Webs that deceive by no pictorial sleights, but
Trompent l'oeil in another way: not imaging things
That seem to be, but building traps that seem not to.

And it is not that I sit now at the center of the whole
Thing, waiting for its delicate strong threads to trap
The stupidly unwary, or to fascinate the clever
Who trace the pattern of its trusswork
And wonder how much its yielding beauty
In a gentle breeze may in itself be a trope
Of a trap, until they too are trapped in that metaphor of a metaphor,
The thing itself, the very thing. It is not that
I sit there, for that minutely dense center
Is a riddling figure of me: all the rest
May be seen as being drawn out of it, as from myself.

No: I sit tight in an upper corner
Regarding my lovely gossamer garden,
Until someone unwise is caught in the toils of my *toile*.
Then he becomes the center
Of my concern, and I wrap my lines about him,
Preserved if not eternized in the cocoon
Of my sonnet. But in time
He will be gone, and my web will break,
And float to and fro in some breeze or other.

And then? As I start out again to spin
A new tale, another jail of voile, another
Geometric wonder, I remember
The face of the Goddess, as I
Affix my prime filament to the right
Place, and begin
To spin, upward as I move down, hanging
Like life itself, after all, by a thread.

FORGET HOW TO REMEMBER
HOW TO FORGET

"I have a rotten memory" began
The American version of that long
French novel: and save for the telling word
Leaping in all its colors out of the
Grayish blank, or for the mad turn of phrase
That I, unyielding judge, committed to
My bedlam memory, I cannot come
Up with exactly what was said even
In a recent conversation. Books can
Remember, for they have written it all
Down—they are in themselves all written down—
And, as Phaedrus was famously told in
That lovely grove (and this was written down),
Writing is remembering's enemy.

Writing it down—thereby writing it up,
The "it" here being language or event—
Allows what was told to recall itself.
The flux of our experience will dry
Into mere flecks; once-great spots of time now
Are filmy moments of place, on the page,
In the full course—or somewhere on the banks—
Of all that streams behind me. And the dear
Name of oh, Whatshername, herself—oh, yes
Mnemosyne (lost for a minute in
An overstuffed, messy drawer, crammed with names)
Is all I have to call on for a guide
To wherever back up the relentless
River I might momently have to go.

And who, when hindsight frays, would want the most
Obvious compensation of foresight,
Prophecy creeping into the places
Recall was slowly vacating? Only

The young with so much to look forward to
And little to remember could call it
A reasonable deal, and better to
Go on climbing, as steps on steps arise
And it all keeps dissolving into that
Father of Waters that every fresh
Moment originates anew, the while
Some sort of sweet, silent judgment commutes
All that, accessible or not, streams out
Behind you into time already served.

GETTING FROM HERE TO THERE

I

After the issues raised first by the dawn
Had been considered for a while and (darn
It!) lost their appeal, some agent of the dark
Stabbed at the afternoon as if with a dirk:
The disappearance of the sun's red disk
In a sea of golden dust brought us to dusk.

One hears such stories with one's eyes unwet:
She woke up one day and found that the Tet
Offensive had left her widowed with a tot
Who broke her heart as if it were a toy.
Luck, having given her one so-so try,
Wrung out her life and left her bones to dry.

How many other questions hide in "how?"
Writers should make a deep, unwitting vow
Never to think about such questions (Wow!
I wish I could!) Rather than try to woo
Answers into the mind's arms, dream of Who,
Where, What they were wearing then, and Why.

She took him to her place at half-past one,
Her bedroom windows bordered by caca d'oie
Chintz draperies—not nice—but lust says fie
To nice, for which it does not give a fig.
He'd gone there Thursday, just for a quick fix,
And didn't get back home till after six.

Wisdom's long weary journey from the east
Ceased when it halted once to take its ease
In some oasis with a book, a vase
Of flowers, a cup of wine, love in a vale

Of silken-covered sand, no weathervane
Clattering, ostentatious, giving vent
To windy thoughts. It knew whereof it went:
The overgoing of the sad, late west.

He misdirected us, and so we came
By a long route, which took us through a cave
Filled with the lapping of a distant wave.
Our confidence already on the wane
We wandered, wondering, ever more in want
Of knowing where the true way really went.

II

He tried to enter but the door was shut
And though he generally tried to shun
Force, still he slammed it hard enough to stun
Anything. Like a film with Anna Sten
Co-starring someone (who?—his name was Sven
Something) the place stank. It was like an oven,
Behind the door he shouldn't have tried to open.

Like the day's weather, starting out with fair
Skies, his finest resolve would finally fail:
The ball, high and well-hit appeared to foil
Despair—(*Let the mare go and save the foal!*
Shouted, quite needlessly, the hopeful fool.)
Then the wind shifted, the ball drifted foul.

Looking up, then: ahead of us, the sky
Behind, the ground that we still somehow shy
Away from, now uncomforted by "thy
Rod and thy staff," parts of a broken toy
We barely even played with as a boy;
And like the most expensive shoes we buy
Our—how do you say it—*esperanza? (muy
Buen!)* starts high but will return to mud.

(What he forgot, in all the heat
Of life, of course went to his head,
The wealth all spent that warmth once held
Now nothing left to give, to hold
Here in the kingdom of the cold.)

III

As the text says, we all start out from dust
And passing through (inevitably!) lust,
We might move right to "dust" again, at last.
But life insists on running through its list
And holding—however knotted up—the line
Passing through this and that, for each a lone
Syllable, with its own peculiar tone
(There is no way in which they form a tune),
Each a fake hieroglyph or misread rune,
Aiding speech in its long-resounding ruse.
Adam's name was as red as that of rust,
The color of our first and lasting dust.

ACROSS THE BOARD

BANG! (the starter's pistol) and we begin.
Whatever you may have staked upon the race
There's something you will have to come to know.

We can hear nothing in the thundering din;
The voice of comment dies without a trace.
No matter what you're saying: there they go!

With Surface scratched (to nobody's chagrin)
The gelding Hope maintains a lightning pace
Beside whom Possibility seems slow.

Now randy Yang pursues the fleeing Yin
Unwitting of the truth we all must face:
Whatever begins in joy will end in woe;

What do they flee from that must be within
Themselves? is it others, or Time they chase,
Hoping to reap what they won't have to sow?

To *"Come back home wid a pocket full ob tin"*
But not quite in the money's no disgrace;
Yet losing's in no way to win, although

We could remark that it all had been
—Given the facts that the particular case
Presented—quite unquestionably *vaut*

Le voyage; as when we go out for a spin
On some grand afternoon and at the base
Of a great hill, we turn, and in the glow

Of sunset, like a map on which we pin
Our hopes we see revealed the recent space
Of the plain we'd just climbed from, far below.

Betting across the board may leave us in
Far deeper trouble than we might by grace
Of circumstance escape from. Even so

Here at the finish, nothing's left to win
Although, surely, something has taken place;
As always, the bottom line is all for show.

VARIATIONS ON A TABLE-TOP

for Saul Steinberg

(Whose carved and painted
Balsa table-tops
Were sculpted drawings
Of the table-tops
They were drawn upon.)

I

The varnished, waxed, mahogany veneer of the table-top
Where he sat, unable to write truthfully of what truth was,
Shone back at him, uninvitingly showing only his own
Reflectiveness, standing for all its wide mirroring of mind.
The plain deal table in the kitchen where the vegetables get
Chopped, stood for nothing but what was rightfully done on it, and
Thereby—how splendidly exemplary this was!—for itself.

Locke's *tabula rasa* was blank only if you couldn't see
The intricate structures of possibility a landscape
Of openness, (imprisoned in contingency nonetheless,
Locked in the very jail of what it could ever be open *to*)
A still-life of quick motionlessness? a tableau vivant of
The heretical panel of *The Creation of the World?*

On the Multiplication Table, X and Y were going
Away at it, following the biblical injunction. But
Was it truly fruitful? alas we ask, (and more and more we
Have to ask). But here is another question, set for us by
That great examiner, Late Morning: Consider that
The discussion of the nasty matter was tabled in Great
Britain, and thereupon the back benchers started to shout, some
At once and others in quick succession, very nasty things.
But on this side of the Atlantic the very same motion
Was tabled and everyone there heaved a great sigh of relief:

What did the respective tables look like? Was the British one
All of metal, or perhaps even tiled, so that whatever
Blood was involved could easily be cleaned up? Was the one in
Washington placed high up on a dusty balcony where few
People ever went, save for the night-watchman, on his sad rounds?
(Be specific. Do not write on more than two sides of the page.)

He lay there at the end of things; what was it he still could see:
A table of green fields, laid out in squares with hedgerows and small
Brooks? Or was it the squares on the quilt he could make out
    beneath
His nose (sharp as a pin? as a pen?) stretching out sadly toward
The distant and inaccessible hills of his covered feet?

II

But Babel crashed in a thunder of wreckage and the mortared
Syntax which held words fast to harder (but no less durable)
Things crumbled into bricky chunks: the world fell into its own
Grand aphasia and we had to make allowances for
Almost everything; still, in the twilight of meaning one could
Glimpse momentary sparks of sense, like the cold and lovely blue-
Green of fireflies benignly but significantly flashing
So that there was at least something to go on. For example
Untwisting the mystery of the Bower of Tabel, the
Lost place of light, highest garden of eloquence—with
The consequence that words like table lost some of their grip on
Things, and neighboring words moved in for the referential kill:

"See here, now! I'm going to lay my cards on the sable!" But
Did he mean the last remaining pelt, let-out, but not needed
For Mrs. Blasenkopf's coat? we knew that whatever he thought, it
Was all shifting sand; meanwhile the less substantial Knights of the
Round Fable were spoken of, told of, as if they had been there;
(Or, if you prefer *arrosto d'Ariosto,* Fancy munched
On the fast food of the open-all-night *favola calda.*)
It was said of the late wise Professor that, young and foolish,
He had a local whore in the Society of Fellows'

Rooms, upon a celebrated and highly-polished Mabel
(As in *"Get off the Mabel, the two bucks is the waiter's tip"*);
Something untoward about the green baize of the billiard gable
Caused all the balls to hasten to the side cushions as if they
Were caught in one of two adjacent gravitational fields;
And when the enraged curmudgeon pounded the unyielding oaken
Stable (but not the sort that had ever even heard of the
Horse), his hand hurt, but we all acknowledged his authority:
The sturdy, old, ugly "golden" oak that had come to him from
Some turn-of-the-century schoolroom quite legibly proclaimed
The contents of his character as he pounded once again
On the label around which sat his intimidated peers.
On the walls above, gazing out over the tedium of
This scene was a faded sepia print that might have been one
Of J.H. Tischmann's *Moses Bearing the Cables of the Law;*

—And so forth. But were these all examples of the very same
Phenomenon? Were they, too, variations on some theme, some
Enigma at the center? (I imagine it lying there
Like some crazy lazy Susan, pre-Copernican, who knew
Just that the table of the world whirled about her fixity).

III

How to turn the tables on these turns of designation, though?
Playing on the name and with the palpable surface itself
Is to play variations "on" it as on a piano
And as on a theme, the motif of itself in its great, flat
Capacity for taking on the work of our minds, our hands,
Our eyes; and taking pen in hand—unmindful that, were it not
For the flat opacity of yielding paper which prevents
Any mirroring of that writing from the table-top, all
Might be lost in the distractions of self-regard—is at last
To climb to the table land and see, not a fancy prospect
As from a mountaintop, or across a bay at sunset, but
Again the broad true plain, ungirded by any lofty hills.

DICKCISSEL

SPIZA AMERICANA *A crossbill. "The black-bibbed male sings from a continuous perch; the sparrow-like female is seldom noticed."*

BIRDS OF NORTH AMERICA

At the edge of my feeder a sparrow would
Sit singing *"cissel, dick-cissel,*
Dick-cissel; I'd have said to him "Dickey-bird, why
Do you sit, singing *'cissel, dick-cissel, dick-*
Cissel'" save that (a) it wasn't a sparrow at
All; but, huddled among the house sparrows all
Having a go at the stuff in the bird-feeder, clearly
Something else—a twisted bill, as if put out
Of joint by some cat in an animated cartoon, a splash of
Yellow surrounding the black on its breast—
No, no sparrow at all; and (b) it wasn't "singing" anything
Like that—like *"dick-cissel"*—but rather
A sort of—well, I suppose that *"tit tit tit brrrssshh"*
Might be one way of putting it, or taking it, for
That matter, freed from the birdcage of American
Speech; or if one must be literary, somewhere
Between *titcissel* and *dickwillow* lies not the sound
Of the bird's call or song but the name
Of its nature, noisy but, when it comes
To language, silent. And at best, I might say or might sing
In Sullivan's music *"Dickcissel, I'll teach you to whistle"*
Or some such song. Yet cut in the bark of its bite, or
Inscribed in its quavers and crotchets there still
Would be nothing to read, no
Epistles of Dick the apostle or even of Paul the
Dickcissel. Nothing but *brrrssshh.*

Now, I'm sure, just as sure
As I'm sure that my name is what it is, that
Absence makes the mind grow yonder; out of height
Is out of heart; one short gulp of summer
Doesn't make a swallow start
In on its autumnal twitter
Though a sparrow fall, or a dickcissel rise
In winter mornings: and after all, where birds have meanings
And names, like all words, wings
And what you lose roundly on the abouts you make up
On the sings until . . .
Well, in for a many, in for a mound
—I, you, Dickcissel, Alf, Ed, everyone—
Of final ground.

X'S SYNDROME

Phi Beta Kappa poem, Yale University, 1996

Quinsy, archaically dogging the throat, the whiffles
(Where did they go?), the glanders poor horses get,
The pip (a disease of chickens), the purely invented
Candlemaker's glottis (by Peter Shaffer
In nineteen fifty-one): these prebiomedical
Names for blights that afflict us afflict us themselves
With a charm and a horror (those unknowns! lying behind
The folksy masks of such names in an aetiological
Void . . .) And even if now, with a greater degree
Of sophistication, still named after a place
The illness appeared to haunt—Tapanuli fever,
The Black Formosa corruption, Madura foot—
And perhaps the citizens of wherever it was
Bleating objections (as if Lyme, say, didn't want
To have its name stigmatized with a spreading disease
That possibly anyway came from deer on Naushon.)

But nature disposes and medical science proposes
Other arrangements of naming: a disease like a rare
Flower is given a crypto-Linnaean name
By its responsible discoverer, as with
A wild surmise he gazes on the specific
Symptom that might be ascribed to Y's disease
Or W's, but given the facts of the case,
Had to be acknowledged as something new.

And so "X's syndrome"—the name of a manifestation,
A race of observable elements of illness
Running together (as if for their health? as if
For the sport of it?); not to be named for even
Some singular victim of its incursions or torments
But for the physician who first distinguished it.

And who was X after all? what story could truth
Tell us of him as a person? What of his childhood?
What beach did he play upon in summer twilight
As the golden sand reddened, grew cold, and the tide receded
Into the menacing dark? Or what fair field
Empty of folk, far from larger bodies of water
Did he gaze across, under a leaden sky?
X: was it always his name? was it shortened from something
Polysyllabic? And what was the name of the journal
He published his great result in? No matter. I quote from The
Paper that brought an entity into the world
By naming it, having established the right to do so:
The patient first presented with longer and longer
Periods of silence, matching the silent prognosis
He was presented with; on alternate days
The fever peaked at dawn or evening twilight . . .
A cessation of speech? a silencing, (a muteation?
—Ha, ha!) that may abate if death does not,
Come first with that other silence of the grave . . .

X's Syndrome. Not ours. The illness is ours:
The disease with its causes and slowly evolving rituals
Of treatment will always have been Dr. X's construction.

But now that I know what it's called, we should be well
On our way to recovery, coming around again,
From what it is we're said to suffer from.

TWO PREDATORS

I

He will acknowledge no fault in himself.
Unlike his prey—or those others who are
At most part of the scenery through which
He pushes his mortal pursuit, he can
Not imagine what in him could demand
Sad scrutiny. And as for those he hunts,
Aswim, a-scampering, a-flap,
Driven on by the terror, chilling, of
Sudden recognition but all too late—
A kind of widespread fault (miscalled by
Those who talk like that a virtue), cruelly
Cripples those he feeds on, the fault of being
Able to perceive that some habit or
Disposition of your own frailty which
Needlessly harms or discomforts others
Is a fault—to be acknowledged as such,
A fault perhaps even to be worked at.
This very awareness in itself he
Knows to be the sick blossom of weak roots
Sent up as if in defense; no more than
A sign that one is destined to be his
Lunch.   As for his own very awareness
That this common phenomenon exists
In others—this self-deception, almost
Sad? He might have to allow, after all,
That this, perhaps, is his only weakness.

II

One of those who, indeed, "talk like that," she
Does not prey on the living beings—not
(She knows as well as she knows anything),
Like him; instead, she says, "The tiny bits
That I graze on are not moved by what gives
You and me our life, motion and being."
Being deeply certain that she is no
Creature of prey, she will consider all
Her lapses and insensitivities,
Sadly, but with some hope that her own mind's
Inner and truthful mirror may reveal
Where, and just how far, she still has to go.
As she bears down on what she knows to be
Her ruminative and benign grazing
(Nature green in hoof and maw) there below
The reach of her consciousness bits of stirred
Consciousness flash out in what will be her
Lunch.
         And see now, how as she swims, wings, strides,
Her oncoming slow motion strikes terror
There in the tiny . . . whatever they are—
Hearts?—of her animated provender.

FANCYING THINGS UP

for Kenneth Gross

O that metal were not so literally
Massive, that stone would have somehow to feign
Solidity, like paint: to seem to be

Alive is all the fiction statues can
Amass, images struck with petrifaction.
Pictures that arise on wings of trope

Can seem to seem, and with that seeming, hope
To figure what in us might better reign
In what will come to be, a truer fiction.

Not marble, but the gilded and corrupted
Metal of public talk, in this our squawking
America, makes up our monuments.

Leaden finalities for which we opted
Make nasty statues of our very gawking,
Thick but unsound, solid but void of sense,

Unbeautiful, quite uninstructive and
Unmoving—to observe the obvious—
In their way, giving the palpable a bad

Name. (Save for when many a passing hand
With many a passing rub has given us
A gleaming nose or toe no sculptor had

In mind.) That might conclude it all. But see—
Long past an age when it might sometimes matter
That even green-patina bronze could weep,

In the cold lap of stone Prosperity,
That statue no high rhetoric could shatter,
The tramp we all are grabs his bit of sleep.

A SHADOW OF A GREAT ROCK
IN A WEARY LAND

Isaiah 32.2

Let him who is without light
Among you cast the first
Shadow, and let the worst
Among us here at our late

Hour now speak for the best:
There is nothing higher above
Our heads, and we whimper of
What once had been our boast.

When among all possessions
Knowledge, alone, is un-
Acknowledged to be one
Of our treasures or our passions.

Failing of wont and of will,
All we construct or construe
In neither sense holds true:
What can we still do well?

Bewail with an outraged heart
Infringements upon what
Is our Divine Right Not
To Have Our Feelings Hurt?

Not even that—the airs
And choruses of complaint
Are poorly intoned, and faint:
They fall on our own deaf ears.

Tell over the old tales
Of the hope from which we grew,
And our fading claims to be new
Now as some curfew tolls?

Not even that—in fear
Of singularity
Blockhead and airhead flee
Transports of metaphor.

Remember what we once were,
Even if too late to learn
How our fattening unconcern
Fed in the troughs of war?

Not even that—our boughs
Broke too soon, too soon
While an affable buffoon
Sang us his lullabies.

Sing in dumb unison—scared
Or ignorant of the joint
Divergence of counterpoint
In which true tunes are scored?

Not even that—our air
Amplifies voicelessness;
The silence of unsuccess
Sighs for all that we are

Still to contrive to succeed
In failing at; we play
At work and labor all day
At play, sad to be said.

That idiot, Paradox, laughed,
For the steps we had to take
To save ourselves would break
The best that we had left—

Those principles we still
Assure ourselves that we
Keep though imperfectly—
The air of assent grows stale,

And harsh the voice of each claim.
Hope and distrust of hope
Are braided together in rope
—To hang ourselves with, or climb

Out of acedia's pit?
There is no sign for us
In the ambiguous
Text of this bubbling pot

In which we seethe as a tame
Curl of smoke ascends
From the burning of candle-ends
That is the fire this time.

The fire that brings to a boil
A terror beyond all fears,
A broth of soured tears
Fills the horizon's bowl,

Loud in such darkness, whether
Soon to be burnt or drowned,
Our dimmed noise and unsound
Light will come together.

THE PARADE

"Some hand in hand, but never, thank God, in step"
W.H. AUDEN, *In Praise of Limestone*

Back in the days when the sound
Of the various different drummers
Pounded out for all comers
The same unchanging command,

To march against Whatever
Or to go limp and be
Dragged off in the piety
Of some general palaver

Was only a cut above
Proclaiming with shows of passion
The hemline length of fashion;
The young then, and the brave

Were no less uniformed
Than armies of their day,
Well-drilled in their own way,
And state-of-the-art well-armed.

Time passed; this did not stop
In our newly benighted land:
Idling "hand in hand"
Is our way of marching in step;

In unison, ragged and loud
That can hardly be
Whitman's polyphony
Of differences that led

A democratic march,
As whatever glory was fades,
Now factional parades
Pass by in a similar lurch.

"Diversity"? A mass
Of various bottled flavors
No national cooking savors
Stewed to a tasteless mess.

"Quality" (what a *Schandeh!*)
When used as an adjective
It now just serves to give
A sign that a whole agenda

Is not to be discussed.
"Street-smarts"? the virtue claimed
By what C. Wright Mills once named
The "crackpot realist"

(As if "experience"
—Dense, Emersonian word—
Had best remain unheard
Though unembarrassing once.)

At the narcissistic lilt,
The jock's swagger, the air-
Head's nods and pouting pair
Of eyebrows with the salt

—Savorless—of affected
Gestures of affection
Empty of indirection,
A mindlessness enacted,

Our good sense flags, and weary
Grows the old quizzical
Frame that held our still
Internalized Missouri.

But "show me" does no good
If I am blind to being
Shown and so unseeing
That plain text reads as code.

Ocular evidence—
If I am blind to what
Is shown and what is not—
Is just the theme of a dance.

What passes for a hale
And hopefully skeptical state
We once felt was innate?
An intellectual *Heil*!

These pound at truth and honor
Like goose-stepping jackboots that
Slap the pavement in flat
Contempt, driven by inner

Emptiness, soft terror.
Look left, look right: the trace
Of sameness blurs each face
In its appalling mirror.

THERE OR THEN

At home, at noon, I am located by three *where*
Coordinates and one for *when* but none
For *late* or *soon* which seems
Unfair: the realm of here and there
Scorns the immense expanse of now and then
With its symmetrical maps: *Then* future
And *then* past are both perhaps
Whenever in time present and *now* negates them both
And like the two-faced mirror of zero that can endow
The integers with negative looks at themselves
Sits always on the threshold between the dark
Bedroom and its corners of remembrance
And the sunny kitchen where the next things are being whipped
Up. Which is also to say that *Now* lies on a curve
Whose values are the relative timelinesses,
Stretching, before our days and beyond our years,
In its own kind of silence. *Late* and *soon*
And—*ready* perhaps?—would frame a sort of space
In which a palpable *now* might take shape
By taking place—by taking one of an infinite
Number of places: the active *Now!* of our most agitated
Imperatives, and not the usual passive one,
Lying about in the sun by the side of the pool
Glomming the fronts and backs of the occasionals, blond
And bland, as they passed, the *now and then*
Moment which, because it can be so readily
Imagined, is so prone to being deferred.
Like the enactment of our resolutions, like—
But only for a limited while—our death.

FIRE!

Poor Phlogiston!—deconstructed
By new paradigms, inductive
Inquiries and Occam's razor
Into what is just a case of
Very rapid oxidation.
Still, we stare into the open
      Fire (Gaston Bachelard

Wrote so well of that), and still we
(Playing with fire?) ply old tropes of
Heat and Light and all those tradeoffs
(Feeling? Knowledge?) that we keep on
Making in our double-dealings
With ourselves, and somehow making
      Sense thereby of how we live.

Instrumental bits of flame that,
Melting, welding, sterilizing,
Cauterizing and annealing,
Help us with our busy, heavy
Handiwork—and not to speak of
One last immolating pyre:
      Ashes crumbling into dust . . .

Not to speak of all the wanting,
All the trembling Sappho said was
Freezing-burning both together;
Five-alarm or less heroic
Nonetheless it can so fiercely
Turn attention into madness,
      Knowledge into ignorance . . .

Not to speak of ancient ardor,
(For God, Country, and etc.)
Nor of *Fire!* shouted in a
Now proverbial crowded theater,
Nor indeed in some bare courtyard,
Chill and empty now of all save
  You and your own rifle-squad, . . .

Nor indeed of those two burnings,
Hunger and his brother Anger;
Not as with us now, but ever
Nibbling at—until consuming
Finally—all of one another,
Each of them, though, fanning very
  Noisily the other's flames.

DIGITAL

I

Thumb: here to press, oppose and
Be opposed: it rhymes with dumb—

Pointer, ostensive speaker and our designator,
author of first signs, truest friend of thumb

Middle, whose very length can sometimes matter far
more than its centrality, hugs pointer in blessing

Ring-bearer, awkward contingent but good for
grasping as well as to be grasped by rings

Little finger, afterthought, appearing
longer, having begun on higher ground

II

We have counted on them
For so long, and to do more and more
Of the work of our lives, starting with
Primitive fingerings in the receding
Dawn of history: cave painting

Pottery, small things
Of bone and stone and who knows what
Modes of caressing (the archaeology of
Love remains swathed in unknowing)
Learning and teaching all the

Languages of contact,
Thereby giving tongue to a silent
Manifold of touch, keeping sceptical
Faith with sight and modulations
Of tiny noises on string and

Pipe. Thus the ear of
The mind might mime their dancing—
Instrumental withal—to the tune of
That very dancing from which they
Will retire in the morning

Light to become mere
Handmaidens of that taskmaster
Manual Labor, who conjoins them in
Communal work which would be
Undone by their loving play.

III

—Which, when fingered styluses took to leading
Hidden thought out into the light of being
Written down, blank pages of spawning words and
        integers breeding,

Integers embodied almost like souls in
Fingers—as in Greek they were designated—
Broke out from their bodily prisons inside
        parts they were wholes in . . .

—Which, when beads of the abacus slapped together
Under fingers clicking like castanets and
Stood for metaphorical digits, dancing
        light as a feather,

Abacus then led to the wheel whose turning
Decimal determination compelled the
Motions of adjacent wheels and no matter
        that all their yearning

Was to rest. Thus hopping of bead gave way to
Thirty-six degrees of a new rotation
As a waltzing algorithm kicked in then,
    leading today to

Bustling whispers—bristling (though hardly horrid)
Work that is much less of the hands and more of
Fingers twisting, flicking, at buttons, keys, the
    mouse's broad forehead . . .

Notice how the literal, though, keeps getting
Out of hand: the busyings of our fingers
Claim the name of work today (but we find this
    thereby upsetting)

(Tropes endure, old falsehoods thereby eroding—
See? our fingers have always come in handy)
Now the old opposable digits' trope of
    binary coding

And its fruitful, terminal oppositions—
On-and-off and falsity/truth—provide the
Newest looms to busy our fingers under
    changing conditions.

IV

But while we hearken to the modeled fable
Of something occurring in the mind, the trip
Of fingers drumming nervously on the table
And something moving in the microchip,

Said microchip unwise, deaf dumb and blind
Usurps our memory, keeps our knowledge for us,
As molecules of what is a kind of mind,
Joining in an infinitesimal chorus,

Expending space while ever keeping time—
Held still without him, set in motion with him—
Sing to the humming of that paradigm,
Dance to the measure of its algorithm.

V

Fingers work now, but in the end they come to
Gradually gather as hands again, while
All that real but endless parade of digits
        marches in sum to

Some infinity or other, while, gamely
Managing the fragile and energetic
Ten that we are right to be left with ask one
        last question namely

Which hand now, the sinister one (or merely
gauche?) or else the dexterous one? whichever
then, the hand we favor must be the right one.
        This is seen clearly

In the scribbling hand of the truly clever
Which death's celebrated and quite unfunny
Bocca della verità will completely
        swallow forever

Any hand that writes or that reaches out to
Grasp some sense at last of the stuff of darkness.
Even hands like ours are quickly withdrawn in
        terror and doubt, too

Soon. In Rome though, do as I've done, and linger
For a while just across the street from Vesta's
Temple, stop, turn back for a moment there and
        give it the finger.

OWL

Phi Beta Kappa poem, Harvard, 1996

Now that the owl-light—in the time between
Dog and wolf, as some call it—ends, we wait
　As you alight on an unseen
　　Branch to interrogate

The listener and the rememberer;
Lost outlines heighten—as last colors fade—
　The sounder darkness you confer
　　Upon the spruce's shade.

Deluded by the noonlight's wide display
Of everything, our vision floats through thin
　Spaces of ill-illumined day:
　　How we are taken in

By what we take in with our roving eyes!
Your constant ones, if moved to track or trace,
　Take their head with them, lantern-wise
　　Taking heed, keeping face

In the society of night, and keeping
Faith with the spirit of pure fixity
　That sets the mind's great heart to leaping
　　At what you more than see.

Medusa's visage gazed our bodies to
Literal stone unshaded: your face, caught
　In our glance widely eyes us through,
　　Astonishing our thought.

You who debated with the nightingale
The rectitude of northern wisdom, cold
　Against the love-stuff of the tale
　　The laid-back south had told;

45

And yet who stood amid the lovely, thick
Leaves of the ivy, while in all their folly
   The larks and thrushes sought the prick
     And berries of the holly;

You who confounded the rapacious crow
Thus to be favored by the great sky-eyed
   Queen of the air and all who know,
     Now ever by her side;

With silent wing and interrogative
Cry in lieu of a merely charming song,
   You sound the dark in which you live
     Perched above right and wrong.

Resonance is not vacancy: although
He could hear nothing in your hollow howls
   But woe and his own guilt, Thoreau
     Rejoiced that there were owls.

Scattered and occasional questionings
With here and there too late a warning shout,
   Wisdom arises on the wings
     Of darkness and of doubt.

Where in day's vastnesses does truth reside?
In noon's uncompromising light and heat
   When even our own shadows hide
     Under our very feet?

Or in the hidden center of the quick
Resilient dark on which your narrowed sight
   So pointedly alights to pick
     Not the day, but the night,

Its fruitful flower, petaled a hundredfold?
Oh it is there, truth, with the poor blind prey
   Trembling with prescience or cold
     Waiting for how your way

Of well-tuned suddenness and certitude
Tight-strung and execution highly wrought
   Leads to the pounced-on object, food
     For something beyond thought,

By overlooking nothing, overseeing
In all the stillness hidden, tiny motions
   Squirming with the life of being
     Inferences and notions.

With patient agency the beak and claws
Of fierce sublime awareness pluck it clean
   Deriving what for us are laws
     Governing the unseen.

Under torn canvas we put out to sea
Trusting, though puzzled by what glows above,
   To something like philosophy
     To be the helmsman of

Life (but whose life?). Your lessons of the land,
Down-to-tree, then, if not-to-earth, indict
   Our helplessness to understand
     Just what we are at night.

Immensities of starlight told us lies
Of what and where we are; but, we allow,
   Drunk with the Milky Way, our eyes
     Are on the Wagon now,

Fugitive slaves, leaving despair for dread
As if in search of the cold, freeing North,
   Keep gazing steadily ahead
    Keep on Keep knowing forth

You urge us, as your silences address
The power that Minerva chose you for:
   Great-winged, far-ranging consciousness
    Now come to rest in your

Olympian attentiveness that finds
The affrighted heartbeat on the ground, perceives
   The flutter of substances, the mind's
    Life in the fallen leaves.

M AND M'S

Tolling through my life like a private bell for
That romantic poet the word "forlorn" felled:
"Muriel" (my mother, her maiden name was
      Muriel Kornfeld)

Kept on showing up in the strangest places,
As if it were echoing some declaiming:
After Mommy, *Muriel*—then what was it?—
      Senators naming

What was then a common cigar whose boxes
Showed an oval frame and—the mere idea
Seemed a bit louche then—an exotic lady
      with a mantilla

Rising high then falling in folds to cover
Most of the fragrant darkness of her hair (a
Fragrance only fancied). It seemed unlikely
      that Habañera

—So I thought her,—ever could have a name like
Muriel, aside from the fact of Mother's
Having somehow staked out a claim . . . no matter,
      then came the others:

Muriel T, the first one: she whom I briefly,
Back when we were fifteen, had gone about with—
Calm, sweet person—she whom I never tried too
      hard to make out with,

Muriel H—O, we were young then, and O
Eheu now, *fugaces labuntur anni*—
Some *Muriel* too, with whom I had seen my very
      first *Don Giovanni;*

Other *Muriel Somethings* (and, incidentally
Spelled the same way—varying jot nor tittle)
Muriel S—I briefly met her once—was
      just a bit brittle;

Muriel M and *Muriel R* were not so
On the other hand, nor *Muriel C* (two
Still alive, one dead now . . .) ma, basta! rather
      let us agree to

Stipulate a catalogue that remains yet
Open-ended: thus with that matter tabled
Now the name itself, rather than a list of
      ladies it labeled . . .

"*Muriel?* my parents like it. I think it's
Welsh and stood for *Miriam*—that's my name in
Hebrew" said my mother one night at dinner
      (not that a layman

In the lore of words and naming might care but,
What if Muri-el had been Hebrew—meaning
What? God's changing?—or, by another route to
      echo the keening

Ever-changing ocean, Muirgheal—Irish,
"Sea-bright"—making a kind of heady sea-brew
Had I known of it then with "mother," but not
      cognate with Hebrew)

Later on it seems in the twelfth and thirteenth
Centuries—named no Irish Undine or fairy
But remained, remember, the Welsh for what in
      English is "Mary,"

"Muriel" became "a favourite name for
English Jewesses, perhaps as a rendered
Form of *Miriam*" (so my learned source says)
    and it engendered,

Surnames—*Merrall, Murrell,* and finally *Merrill*
—Here my stupid, spell-checker, grimly playing
Cat-and-mouse with all of my best intentions,
    ever displaying

Mindless zeal (that dummy! when scanning even
"Muriel" in singular or in plural
Walled up in its ignorance strongly wished to
    change it to "mural")

But somehow, now that it had encountered *"Merrill,"*
Righting my "error," raised the important questions:
"Merlin" "Merit" "Merrily"—then adding
    "(end of suggestions)"

Got it right, though—as JM would indeed have
Noticed. Shouldn't it have suggested "Mirror"
Too, the product (Steven Meyer opined) of
    Merrill and *error?*

And in re all this—Franklin Hollander, my
Father (loose ends, here, but I'll try to tie 'em
Up at last), my Hebrew name being Jocha-
    nan ben Efrayim,

Was of course named *Ephraim,* and of course so
Was my mother *Muriel*'s Dad, the "E" in
His name—it was Alfred E Kornfeld (is there
    something to see, in

This? I wonder now)—being *"Ephraim"* as
Well. *The Book of Ephraim*—I remember
Him, too, living; *Muriel* (Mother) dying
     late in September

'Ninety-four, my friend half a year thereafter,
(Count years now at what has become your peril)
Losses all affiliate other losses:
     Muriel . . . Merrill

Now Time's eye observes of this tale that something
Got both lost and found in the very telling
Ending in these side-by-side names that look now
     like a misspelling

Each one of the other. She laughs, and as for
Him . . . he must be saying "This much, you see, would
Never have been fitted together but for
     me" and his glee-wood

(Not the old harp smitten upon by Anglo-
Saxon scops, but his resonating lyre of
Polished wood that with "yes" and "no" and letters
     echoes the fire of

Inwardness, the mirror of far beyondness
Source of light and shadow at once) agreeing.
Somewhere in the listening darkness now that
     saying and seeing

Have so altered, there in the sky where stars still
Dance and breed, continuous recreation,
Two bright novae seem to have formed tonight a
     new constellation.

FIGUREHEAD

Wondering whether the position you had just taken
On some important question had actually been the best one with
    which to put
It into the right-field seats, or even been something more than a pose
Which betrayed the cracks in the armature holding it up,
You come to the end of the crowded, noisy produce market,
huddled under its shadowing arcades, and turn
Onto the wide street of the docks, suddenly emptied
Of darkness and of the peculiar vacancy of the busy—

And there, there the masts!
Pointing upward into an air now open for availability
Half-concealed in the balance of their rigging,
With ultimate bowsprits doing their ghostly business of unwitting
Assertion, while purporting only to stay, saying
Here, here, forward, forward, this is where we are headed
Whether for good or ill,
The while the mastheads, hardly tokens of steadfastness
When it comes to remaining upright, spar-crossed with yards that
    in turn
Do crazy turns in re the horizon, all thrill with contingency.

But only as you move in closely to this hull or that
One, beginning to decipher the forms of what you had remembered
Schematically, do the carved wooden personages rise into view.
And you pause at her, let us say, newly painted and pointed
Up and away in the quiet noontide sunlight,
Like an afterthought then put forward, or as if a leading idea,
A name or a kind of flag had then formed a ship in its image,
Or else at another time when moonlight refigures her features
When she seems to be something the ship she leaps out of has dreamt.

Does she embody a what, or merely a who?
The horse's head of a Phoenician vessel, the Dutch or English lion,
    a Spanish

Member of the *familia sagrada,* Neptune himself—as if the life
Of the frail bark he leaps forth from were merely on loan from him,
Or perhaps a nautonymous weeping Niobe, or an image of the
    stolid Hope,
Wife of the owner and master, and thus *who* and *what* at once?
Whatever . . . Thrusting out over the water of whatever is to come,
She says:

"Since I am all up front and there is nothing ulterior
About my position, I maintain a high view; not forward, but
Over and through and ever moving
Toward the beyond; I do not have
To scorn the trivial elevation above me of the servile bowsprit
Or ignore the dolphin-striker's silly verticality
Nor, indeed, accept your misconstruction of me as
A legless logo, a figure truncate and wordless
And narrowly emblematic—that being far from my true point,
    which is this:
That when I am no longer above it all, then the state of the ship
Is in trouble, like a nation in deep water, or a bridge engulfed
By what it had been intended to overleap, or the leaf
Of a single life fallen to final ground.

And when I have truly descended,
Not to return, unperturbed, from even the terrible wave,
Shedding all evidence of its devouring rage,
However I may have been in a false position, however
I may have been deceived about the force of prominence,
There are no stems nor sterns
In the sublime inversions of depth from which I and my timbers
—Mine, even if I am only theirs—shall never fall to floating
And treacherous surfaces again."

AN OLD IMAGE (ALCIATI'S EMBLEM #165)

At night the dog, as if it were a mirror,
Gazes at the moon, and seeing himself,
Believes another dog is in it, there;
He barks, but all in vain as his unheeded
Voice is carried off by the winds, and dread
Diana, deaf, continues in her course.

Poor doggie! But that's where we all are, *nicht wahr?*
—Or so the old nattering about ourselves
As seen in the natural mirror of all the dear
And all the dire beasts
Would have it: but two ways of translating
The dusty wisdom of Latin remain—for those
Of us, anyway, who are versed in the living versions
Of crumbling monuments.
We could write "in" or "on," for to see yourself "in"
A mirror means "on" it—on its thinnest and most
Brilliantly self-denying of surfaces;
So that seeing yourself
Truly "in" it is to have seen something
More deeply found and more profound—as in
The trick-and-fun-fair mirrors of our language.

And, with regard to those beasts:
We see our own faults deeply, not on them nor even
In them—they are so marvelously opaque—
But deep at the heart of our knowledge of them, however
Faulty, wrong, twisted or bumpy it may be,
However imperfect, as is our adamic knowledge
Of our compassionate eves, in whatever false
Paradise we may momently feel we are in,
Even as darkness falls.

We gaze upon her; but who could ever look into
Diana, all coldness, unknowing and unknown:
Unpossessed ever, there being
Nothing inside this high phenomenon that
Gave or received the warming of penetration,
Her "silver" mirroring occurring in glitz
And darts; a foil for the "golden" sunlight, indeed, but
Returning nothing of the look of the world to the world's
Gaze, returning nothing
But the doggie's delusions, nothing but our composite
Monsters of image, half made, half made-out in all that bright,
Unblinding, but madly derivative
Light. A cautionary farce of reflectiveness.

We are more—as we come
To know it more, its soft infinite depths—
And see more of our old self-seeking selves,
In the profoundest mirror of the darkness.

EMBLEM

A one-legged woman pointing leftward with one of
her crutches A big knife cutting into the handle
of an even larger one An hour-glass set parallel
to the ground its two cups of sand now framing a
strange pair of beaches A lute that stands up in
the corner of a room, but upside-down, eyeing us
out of the rose in its belly Cupid stealing that
bright mirror his mother Venus stared at herself
in Eulalos a youth condemned for an unstated act
to stand a few feet behind Sisyphus as he starts
on his roll, to tell him that this time the rock
would stay there Here two of the three Disgraces
Schande and Vergogna dancing listlessly about as
the third whose name cannot be uttered sulks The
whole idea was that the picture hit you wham and
then you were told what meaning you had been hit
with only later on and down below in the labored
explications of some Latin verses There it might
appear that the mirror was not that of Venus but
of Vanitas or Veritas perhaps or that your hopes
for some interpretation of the peculiarly shaped
hill say toward which the woman's crutch pointed
would be gratified by the lust of verse to gloss
explain rescue the truth from the merely visible

But see how those high-sailing hopes are
    dashed against the rocks of tedious
and clichéd homily Images that love to depict
    uncanniness fall victim to the moralizing
words that want to make home truths out of
    strange sights And those words which
have the nobler task of making the invisible
    just that much harder to ignore are
set to the menial task of making an old saw
    out of an energetically framed visual
enigma But if these very verses caught sight
    of themselves in a mirror what would
they see And should the Image perceive
    that it was composed of the same pixels of
typed character---here Courier---that
    constitute Text what would it have to say

TWO GLOSSES ON RENÉ MAGRITTE

PRIVATE PARTS

You say you love my X my two Y's, my
Mysterious (as in French or British) Zed;
You quote *Of hand, of foot, of lip, of eye,*
Of brow as if such blazoning—instead

Of blasting persons into smithereens—
Recalled more rightly my embodied ghost
Haunting your sad, hot longing's briefest scenes,
Framed souvenirs of what you thought of most.

Here are these of me: they throw back at you
The melting gaze of all the body's faces
(*Those parts of me that the world's eye doth view*
—Shakespeare again): one person, now five places.

Some Belgian body lacking any right
(As she'd have in America) to bear
Arms—to embrace, surrender with, invite
Or reach up with to rearrange her hair,

Here's your last wet dream painted on the wall,
Looking as if she were contrived by written
Language with all its parts of speech to fall
Apart into chapters, scenes, episodes bitten

Off, short stanzas chopped out of desire's
Longest unbroken melismatic sighs:
Averted gaze and disconnected feet,
Complete and bushy belly, partial thighs

And so on—up and down—each with the stigma
Of unity departed in a pun;
Not present absences, a French enigma,
But rather Greek, of the Many and the One,

Hung in the gallery for all eyeing hearts
Eternal Evidence, but if so, of what?
Parts of my picture? Picture of my parts?
The treason of his images (*This Is Not*

A Body) painted by a man although unseen,
Wearing—a man of parts—a bowler hat.
The sum is greater than the holes between
Its various somethings. That's enough of that.

PAINTED MODEL

Painters being feigners of presence anyway
Any Pygmalion story about a figure
Stepping out of the surface of a canvas
To embrace her love-starved creator would be sleaze.

And so you'd call this *Desire's Hologram*
Only if you'd not thought about what painting
Is, nor felt the lust of representation . . .

But look at him and just what he is doing:
Painting his model—yes, but in every sense
As painting [1] simply (*simply?*) a "picture"
[2] a "picture of" a tree (or lady
Or path through the woods or of the artist himself
"As" Hercules at the crossroads having to choose
Between the competing claims of X and Y.
[3] the side of a barn—the main point being

To get it all covered. But in our case, there
She stands, (not yet?) complete, her skin and hair
Already undercoated with a bright
Invisibility, barely awaiting
The final application of whatever
Will summon up tactility as well
[4] your face at the mirror with a *schmier* of rouge . . .
For after all, this is poetry, a matter
Of the strongest highest and subtlest make-up

The painter's brush consumes his dream proclaimed
The vatic Yeats, and wrong again; for here,
In this clear realm of gaze and wish
His dream is being nourished by his brush.

SUN IN AN EMPTY ROOM
(EDWARD HOPPER)

Early sunlight, even if at a late
Time, enters and plasters itself in the trapezoids
Outlined in shadow—as if given substance thereby—
Along a reach of wall, then significantly echoed
Again, in small, along
A larger reach, as if in memory or in afterthought
Or in some mode of light's picturing of light as it
Composes a picture of the way we know and
Remember and represent (and thus tables of the law
Of light? if so, then to be broken later
In the disappointing day and given again
Only in shadows and other representations).

It may recall an earlier glimpse of emptiness, a corner
Of a room by the sea, opening seemingly
Onto an uncontainable expanse of ocean.
If so, it is almost as if to call up and purify
Such a recollection that this place
Is full, so full, of vacancy. No doubt,
A mind can be preoccupied with light
Like that which occupies a room on a daily basis;
And to look at the most uneventful morning's slow spectacle
—As if through those aids to vision that used to be called
Spectacles themselves—can be to dwell
On the way light can know a room even
As Adam knew Eve in the first room that was all
Outdoors, and full of sufficiency, empty
Of the furniture by which culture copes with nature.
It is as if sheer room had taught us "thus to ruminate,
That time will come" and take our light away, of course; but more:
That the extraordinary can be something less
Than is provided by the clutter of incident.

That it can dwell in the traces of meaningfullness,
Those trapezoidal evidences of the light by which we see the light
We see—*"in lumine tuo videbimus*
Lumen"—(as we might say to the fathering sun what we had once
Sung to the fostering mother of knowledge,
"In thy radiance we see light.")

But for now, we acknowledge
The light of the world into which it has itself been
Thrown. And to ask our selves what we are *doing*
In this space—invading it with our inquiry,
Occupying ourselves not in the literal fictive painted space,
But with a place of contemplation—
We may finally say that, like the painter,
It was ourselves that we were after,
Filled with the minding of the light that dwells
In the inexhaustible flatness of painted
Room, of what we stand before.

ERASING A BAD NAME

Shabriri is the name of a Demon of
Blindness among some Sephardic Jews,
recited in a spell: as the name
disappears, so the demon, and the
condition as well.

SHABRIRI

I'll try this, darkly sceptical, to query
The worth of such logosomatic theory:

———ABRIRI!

My eyes are smarting now, and rather teary . . .

———RIRI!

That blanc is growing thin and weary . . .

———RI!

There now, I can see.

But what if we reversed it? Would a Light
Far beyond seeing give me more than sight?

SHABRI!

(*Mirabile visu!* can this then be me?
I can see now what eye can never see!)

SHAB!

(Being now able to see seeing
itself, is like a state of being.)

SH!

The end now need not be violent;
"*Whereof . . . speak, thereof . . . silent.*"

Charles Sheeler, American, 1883–1965, *The Artist Looks at Nature*, oil on canvas, 1943, 53.3 x 45.7 cm. Gift of the Society for Contemporary American Art, 1944.32. Photograph © 1988, The Art Institute of Chicago, All Rights Reserved.

CHARLES SHEELER'S
THE ARTIST LOOKS AT NATURE (1943)

He paints what he sees, seeing what he paints.

What our eye takes from the scene of his eye
Taking what it does from his photograph,
Taken itself in, and of, the room, takes
Visual counsel from another kind
Of otherness: the eyeing mind and the
Reminded eye are all their own *plein-air.*

It is all so natural: no magic
Of word becoming unlikely image
Here puzzles the very clarity of
Everything in which it all shapes up (like
Magritte's locomotive, say, out of scale,
Emerging from the empty fireplace
As from some sort of invisible, short
Tunnel through third-dimensionality,
Running on time—but not on tracks—in space,
We had been looking at a while ago.)

No. The puzzle here is only the one
Always lurking on the flip side of the
Flat, deep *there* of our gaze: the thingness
Of the picture, the so pictorial
Nature of the thing, the indoors the eye
Is always in whatever the outdoors,
The *camera chiara* of whatever room—
Indoors, outdoors, virtual space, the flat
Or roughened pleasant lands of picture-plane
Unshadowed by any modelling, on
(And, thereby, in) which all the forms can live
And move and have their sort of being—that
Painting can provide.

Yes, an easy joke
Is still there to read: the large landscape of
The *Campagna* being painted away
At in the studio in Rome, or at
Home in the North, is no more or less done
Dal Vero—from nature—than what Sheeler's
Sheeler is doing in this place. (A man's
Studio is his castle, I suppose,
And real artists are always working from
The battlements, even when the easel's
Base implies a spatial pun upon the
Carpet of lawn both flush with and below
The parapet.) The painter's place makes up
Its own space, and the world drops down, drops up
And back away from it in the crazy
Almost Sienese perspective that the
Solid orthogonals of the painted
Interior with Stove have made mock of.

We contemplate, in the painted painting
So tonal it recalls a photograph,
The high, dark stovepipe pointing into as
Much of an upward as the easel's post—
High in a green sea of grassy air, at
One less remove here from the Palpable—
To which it alludes: the artist at work
Overlooks not a forest of symbols
But a field of signs. And what he paints are
Signs—as if road-signs pointing *in* or *out*—
Within or quite beyond ourselves—rather
Than *this way* to *Wimberby, three more miles.*
Yet the ambitious paintings—histories,
The loves of Jove, scenes from the life of Christ,
Portraits, still-lives, pictures of forms and marks
And voids, maps of virtual space, glimpses
Of rooms and, of course, landscapes: no matter
How noble or base fashion may rank them
Are all—in our fashionable patter—
Painted signs (and works by masters are—in

An old-fashioned patter—signed all over).
But then, the very work of painting signs
Itself, the shadow of the act falling
Across the surface of the fictive veil
That gives our eyes access to the room and
Prevents our touch—*Don't even think of it!*—
From verifying its tall tale of depth:
That alien form on the pictured picture?
—The shadow of the hand of the mind's eye.

The eye does its own kind of painting first:
(In vivid illustration of this, see
Morandi painting the surfaces of
His pots, then placing them in a still-life
Set-up and painting them—in another
Sense—again—painting as making and as
Representing.) And so with "landscape": a scene,
A scene as seen, a painting of just that.

Why not paint painting—painting itself—then?
The Odyssey is as natural, as
Much part of what's out there, as the profound
Aegean Sea is; so is Sheeler's picture
Done from the natural, the photograph:
So when he comes at length its parts to frame
Nature and painting are to him the same.

The *nature* of painting? Its inner truth
Is the namesake of its totality
Of objects: true to art is true to both.
Our marks are sounded in a sea of talk:
Thus, perhaps, we shorten pencil into
Pen and figuratively illustrate
Sheeler's bright aphoristical remarks
On the nature of representation
And the representation of nature.

The painting says: *Figure it out yourself.*

WHAT THE LOVERS
IN THE OLD SONGS THOUGHT

Thinking "In the beginning was the—(*What??*)"
Faust tried, for openers, *Wort . . . Sinn . . . Kraft . . . Tat*
("Word"? Meaning? Power?—all these reeked of creed:
He finally settled simply on "the Deed".)
But none of these would do for true Beginning:
Our ghosts were there before all those, and not
Playing love's game in which there is no winning,
But doing love's work, continuous creation
Of all the celebrated lovers' tales,
Of all the letters, all the conversation,
All the strange fictions that plain fact entails
And all the silences that bridge the void
Of words exhausted. Let us take possession
Of Origin, then like some crafty Freud
Saying "In the beginning was Repression"
Or like some cabbalist "First was the Name"
What could we literary lovers claim?

In the beginning was unlikeness? (*Good!*)
In the beginning was the opened door
Through which crept in the soul of all our sins?
In the beginning there was need for more?
In the beginning there was likelihood?—
The oldest gospel of our lives begins
"In the beginning there was metaphor."

LONG AFTER

That spring they fell in love but then—
Things being as they are—that fall,
Fell down, and out of it again.

Surely the odds were more than ten
To one that this would be, as all
That spring they fell in love. But then

That looks so simple, even when
Type-cast, as in the font of small
Clichés like "out of it"; again,

We never "rise" in love (though men
In lust are said to), but must "fall":
That spring they fell in love but then

As love falls into what a pen
Can catch too neatly in its scrawl,
Fell down and out of it again

—Dynamics far beyond our ken
(Could one fall up, in the long haul?)
That spring they fell in love but then
Fell down and out of it again.

GHAZAL: THE SHADE OF THE AUTHOR OF *INDIAN LOVE LYRICS* SPEAKS

For Agha Shahid Ali

Less than the dust beneath (O hear her plea tonight!)
Thy chariot wheel, is one of low degree tonight.

Less than the weed that grows beside thy door.
Even less am I, smaller yet than wee tonight.

Less than the rust that—never mind the rest:
All the tarnished similes agree tonight.

Imprisoned in pre-post-colonial drivel
How shall embracing darkness set me free tonight?

Through the dark courtyard, shall I silently
Make my escape when you get up to pee tonight?

Cut loose now from its mooring my sad dhow,
Shall I let it drift westward from your quay tonight?

I, whose submissive silence hid my heart,
Laugh and sing like the Miller of the Dee tonight

The fountain plashes and the bulbul trills
(I shall go mad if I don't get some zee tonight)

Alas, my lonely cup is cold and dry
No longer tea for two and two for tea tonight

A mightier ruler soon shall have me, his
All-conquering hand shall yet caress my knee tonight.

I welcome him. Farewell, Zahiruddin:
I beg no crumb, I make no final plea tonight

To make it keen and bright, behold how I
Take here thy sword and grease it up with ghee tonight.

Poor hopeless Laurence! Now, Love's last reward,
Death comes for Mrs. Nicholson (that's me) tonight.

THEN ALL SMILES STOPPED TOGETHER

I heard that. Silent pictures listen in
Silence to what is uttered near them, kin
To household spies, or servants. And they learn
How to respond, shadows that can return
More than mere echoes. Pictures publicly
Displayed hear endless hours of drivel; I
Can listen only when the stakes are high,
However, and my curtain drawn aside,
(I am as wide-eared then as narrow-eyed)
For privileged observers few of whom
Could ever hear my discourse. In this room
He has been telling tales of me, but so
—How shall I say it?—curled—that one could know
Nothing of truth, blinded by the display
Of pied surmises flowering from it—Stay,
Too, listener, invisible, of course
To me, and hearken to what is, perforce,
A kind of speaking picture who was once
A mute poem, quite unable to declare
Even her genre. *Looking as if I were
Alive*—Did he mean me as vividly limned
And shadowed image, or the yet-undimmed
Duchess, then only somewhat recently
Defunct? I, the painted figure, or she,
The stilled, smiling, subject?
                                        As for that
—I mean, the "glance" he spoke of—was it at
No one that I was smiling—was it merely
A matter of my smiling heart that clearly
Leapt through my eyes and on to canvas, by-
Passing anything of the mouth, to lie
In paint shadowed across a shadowed face
(Then was no outward smile, and no disgrace
To him, or me, or other), and that heart
Too soon made sad had brightened as if art

Had given life to images that lay
Entombed within it, quickened for a day?
But no. He was no fool, or at least not
That kind of fool. Or was it that a spot
Of pleasure quite unblushing, answering
A gaze of strong acknowledgment, a sting
Of recognition could be less than rash,
My own gaze having caught a sudden flash
Of something lovely yet somehow unknown?
—A face? yes, then I saw it was my own
Gleaming out from a glass hung on the wall
Behind old Pandolf? Or was it that "old
Pandolf" had felt some stirring in his cold
Loins, an abandoned and forgotten fire
That yet could warm them into young desire
And, reaching to adjust the mantle's sprawl
Across my wrist his hand touching hand could fall,
A near-caressing stroke, and linger there
Like his slow brush across my painted, bare
Shoulder? My blush had been one of surprise
Mingled with pity for his folly. Eyes
For Frà Pandolf? No more than could he
Have hands, so wedded to his brush, for me.

What brisk *romanza* would he have that my
Shadowy self should tell? Some household spy
Perhaps who might have put it in his mind
That one—some cousin—stood all day behind
The curtain drawn across the painted scene
Of Mars and Venus on the wall, whose green
Velvety folds parted so that his gaze
Met mine in mid-glance there, and in a maze
Of intertwining eye-beams soon became
A braided rope of feeling vision and
Of seeing touch in light's caressing hand?
Or those "commands" he gave: a word—or ten,
At most, to some poor under-Thing who then
Ordained in turn that Something lower still
Should tell—and down the leaden chain until

It reached that churl, that mere utensil (what
Was his name—*Tiralcollo?*—perhaps not)
To poison me?
         How would it go from there—
That he—the cousin—then, endowed with rare
Knowledge, and with a sure unswerving will
Dispatched the knave, and while I lay there still
Just breathing, he poured down my silent throat
The *aqua vitae* of an antidote?
Or was I stabbed, perhaps, by yet one more
Utensil, in which case—not as before—
We paid him well to substitute (Oh yes,
Sparafucile, that was it) in dress
Of mine the body of a village girl
Hacked up past recognition, the great pearl
You gave me, richly glowing clasped about
Her neck; she'd died the previous week without
A consecrated bed of earth, by her
Own hand? And why not she? for, like Lucrece
She'd been dishonored and had sought her peace
In death; Lucrece belated; thus, the dead
Poor creature being shown him, had he said
*"Cover her face. Mine eyes can dazzle but
At what Frà Pandolf painted"* as they shut
The coffin's eyeless lid? but was he then
Beyond our care and we beyond his ken?

—But never mind the rest. There was no *"you"*
Even to hear me speak of you, no true
Living embodiment of what you feared
—Or hoped?—some younger lover you could beard
There in his den, or mine, no plot, no wild
Escapes across the marshes of a sort
Fit for the blowzy tales of suffered tort
And tortured engines of revenge you read
Too many of, and in your fancy bred
Nothing but shadows of a maddened, hard
Jealousy and deep lack of self-regard.
Ferrara undid me not—there was no smile

But only the painted shadow of a smile
Frà Pandolf, no more lustful than a stone,
Wrought for the sake of shadowing alone,
The false depiction of his pencil, and
No One, no Other, no advancing hand
Across my shoulder or, doubtingthomas-like
To touch my real smile, and therein to strike
Some chord of feeling. I betook myself—
A treasure ring off the shelf—
Alone, out of the palace one dark night,
Quietly and in neither haste nor fright
Rode to a village, then across the plain
A week, to this religious house, whose chain
I gladly slipped beneath, where I have long
Remained, untouched by real or fancied wrong.

But to match Pandolf's lying pencil, then,
The hasty fiction of my truthful pen
Scratches away, the convent cell about
Me that I walled myself within: without,
A flat and weary landscape giving a
Hint of the glooms of marshy Mantova
And all its silences—stillest of all,
The image left behind me on the wall
And prattling of it (I can almost hear
Him now) to some annoyed, impatient ear,
The mad fool, walled up in his rotting pile
Less free than I; at which I truly smile.

AN AFTERWORD

After years of talking of what, in sum (to
Put it bluntly—or sharply), was what one couldn't
Say, of knowing what should or not be known, yes
    now it has come to

All the day's last end that in fact we never
Had to, got to, speak of. Now time has taken
One negating *n* away, that will make it
    now that we ever

Will have. Space is narrower now, and timing
Off; what forms my aftertalk could assume would
Never seem appropriate to your silence:
    hollowly rhyming,

Dulled and always solidly leaden, fragile
Speechlessness that endless and adamantine
Negatives it tries to mimick make seem too
    noisy and agile.

Now the sunlight, golden before the dawning
Red, extended bravely, of utter night; and
Then our sleep fending off what follows, like an
    opening awning.

Great black swan and peacock of blue assemble
While the splendid phoenix of memory rises
Where the waning daylight itself has started
    barely to tremble;

Wide of wing the hovering hawk still flying
Through the living twilight of figuration;
Dark, the night that cancels all seeming; and so
    literal, dying.

Poetry must either become insane or
Shun the strictly literal like the—should we
Say?—the plague, applying a pure and constant
        torque to the plainer

Truth—though we envision the gleaming height of
This or that, the truth we will tumble down to,
Heavy flight of heavenly life once landed.
        Here in the light of

Clear, dull fact now falling on wintry meadows,
All our plainest speaking—calling a spade a
Spade that digs the grave of its own contingent
        whispering shadows—

Might as well be merely the bleat of herded
Souls in feeble parables aimed away from
Everything that is the case, when the world is
        finally unworded.

The way we die then strangely fashions the way we
Live now; and though crawling along the contours
All such once and future grounding presents is
        safer, yet say we

Rather live with a kind of tame abandon
Hoping that *one's personal life is more or
Less* a satire—Kierkegaard once remarked—*on
        poetry and on*

Oneself: and though poetical living sours
At its most wretched, poetry yet can leave us
Not the poisonous fruit of evil, but its
        wonderful flowers

Pressed, but still unwithered between the pages
Come upon with mildly astonished pleasure,
Programme souvenirs that attested we were
        acting our ages.

There's no reaching through any final curtain
With some last word, adding a participle
Hoping to extend its reach by a single
        weak and uncertain

Final syllable, and we send instead this
One last letter which, like a sealed up grave is
Only to be opened—and then, once only—
        after you're dead.

EARLY BIRDS

George Moran, 1883–1949

"The early bird catches the worm"
—A well-known turn Moran and Mack,
The celebrated Two Black Crows of
Vaudeville, were so famous for
Back then in an earlier peaceful
Time when Peace held Righteousness in
Chains, (as she yet tends to do,
While Truth and Mercy battle it out—
See Psalm eighty-five verse ten) But
Who cares about psalms anyway?

And as for that early bird? I see
The 17 year old boy I was
Adrift one languid summer in
L.A., working from time to time
As an incompetent soda-jerk,
Or pearl-diver, equally
Bumbling, at the Pig 'n Whistle
Downtown (residues of morning
Oatmeal and of barley soup—
Those were the messiest to clean)
Or not working, the while living at
The Hotel Barbara at Sixth
And Alvarado—then a shabby,
Peaceful, not unrighteous spot—
By MacArthur Park, where "ruby
And white belamped" the pedaled boats
(I wrote then) would move quietly
On the pond there every evening,
Going to the movies sometimes
Twice a day, hanging about,
Sometimes playing for an hour
An old upright in a place that
Rented time in practice-rooms.

Sometimes eating late at night down
At the corner greasy spoon,
Radiant in the quiet darkness.
Whispering by the Harmonicats
And Bunny Berrigan's *I Can't*
Get Started, playing over and
Over again and not too loudly
On the juke-box.
                In my first week
There, one night I found myself
At the counter next to someone
I had seen from time to time
In the Hotel Barbara's lobby:
An old man, short, with thin white hair
Said his name was George Moran and
That he used to be in vaudeville.

This was nineteen forty-seven
And you could still find extremely
Ancillary vaudeville acts at
Some of the big downtown movie
Theaters in the largest cities
—And in fact I had just seen one
In Chicago, on the way out
To the west coast earlier that
Summer: Basil *Rathbone!?* Sherlock
Holmes in flicks and on the radio!?
Having to stand there and do some
Mindless turn at the Pantages
In the afternoon with hardly
Anyone to see it?—but the
Boy I was preferred not then to
Think about it. Yet I had heard of
Vaudeville in its grander days:
My mother would at dinner run
Through parts of a number of
Gallagher and Sheehan routines
—*What, the lady Mr. Gallagher?*
No, the rowboat Mr. Sheehan

(What lines could have led to that:
Then I rowed her all aroun'
Until finally she went down?
—Surely not in those days) through
Smith and Dale, *"And vas you dere,*
Charlie," also bits from something
Called The Avon Comedy Four
(It was Smith and Dale with two
Ever changing others through the
Years, or so I later learned).

But nobody ever mentioned
"Two Black Crows," Moran & Mack,
And so it was by inference
That all the old man spoke of to me
On those hot, un-airconditioned
Summer nights could come into some
Sort of picture. We would meet
Night after night, save for the few
Occasions when I worked late, or, more
Often when—without a job—I'd
Spend a whole day moving from one
Nth-run fleabag movie theater
To another; he would talk then—
The old man—about the way it
Was; about their act—his and
Charlie Mack's (Mack died in nineteen
Thirty-four: thereafter there were
Various Macks successively);
About their numbers, done in blackface,
Sometimes munching on a melon:
The one about the early bird, the
One about the horses, black and
White (and decades later I
Came to recall this in the midst of
Reading of how T. S. Eliot
Had by heart Moran and Mack's
Routine about a lion-tamer
Which he went through with belated

Gusto). As the weeks went by he
Showed me, there in his room
At the hotel Barbara

—"Barbara," yes: that was the name of
My first love, whom I would get to
Meet the following winter in New
York, but that's a souvenir
In some wholly other story—

Boxes of memorabilia
Programs, billings, photographs,
And cranked up on a portable
Victrola (as they then were often
Called) ten-inch shellac recordings
(That's what "disks" meant then) of
Several Two Black Crows routines and
Gave the boy a glossy photo:
Himself posing, not in blackface,
With one or another of the
Later Macks. And as the weeks went
By he told me, too, of what his
Life had been: his name was Searcy;
He'd been married, had a daughter
Living with her mother's Jewish
And protective family in
Queens—Claire White (Weiss, probably, I'd
Now guess) she had been a showgirl
Working in Earl Carroll's famous
Vanities when Two Black Crows were
Featured in it; they had married
Had a daughter and divorced in
Nineteen thirty-eight. He hadn't
Seen his daughter for so many
Years; the family weren't speaking
To him. Finally, if and when
I went back to New York—for, the
End of August creeping up, it
Now appeared I would indeed

Leave the Hotel Barbara, the
Lake, the desultory week-long
Jobs, the quiet colloquies at
Night with George Moran, to travel
Eastward home and give the over-
Travelled path another try—
Would I then look up the daughter?
Would I write him that I'd seen her?

Well, in fact, this is what happened
(I could far too easily have
Added that the facts themselves
Rang all untrue, like the ending
Of a typical short story
Of the sad, deflating sort): the
Boy I was gave up the ghost of
What had prompted him to wander
Westward, wired home for money,
Returned to school before September;
Put aside the mad and hazy
Idleness in which I'd slumbered
All that peaceable withal yet
Deeply troubling young summer;
After a brief glance or two at
The Queens telephone book; after
Trying to imagine how I
Might find the address—and then?
Telephoning? No—the family
Wouldn't, I'd supposed, allow that
Even if they could believe my
Story; after a few weekly
Weakening resolves to try to find her;
After that, well, nothing, save for
One short letter sent from
Somewhere in the north—I'd answered,
Saying nothing of the mission—
Then more nothing in the way of further
Contact. That in fact was it.

I would rather (and I do not
Speak now for that boy today, but
Only for myself) that truths were
Told about the kind of quest
That might have been set out on by
Sir Boy on his nightly errand
Taking him on bus and subway
Routes through Queens (Kew Gardens? Forest
Hills, along the Independent
Subway, clean and speedy then?—no,
Rather too grand—maybe Flushing?
But in any case the man who
Was the boy has quite forgotten
Just exactly where he'd thought the
Girl Moran would now be living)
But in any case that didn't
Matter—undergoing minor
Trials, undoing many knitted-
Up enigmas, he would find them,
Rescuing the Girl (his age) from
Mama Ignorance and Grandma
Fear, and taking her to play with
Him in the accelerating
Energies of New York City
In an age of still unrighteous
Peace in nineteen forty-seven
That was how the story ended.

George Moran was sixty-seven
When he died (I now discover
Now that I am also sixty-
Seven) in a charity hospital
In—and thereby might there not have
Been at least this bit of *there* there?
—Oakland. This, the boy then in the
Flat unmoving heat of August
In New York just two years later
Read in an obituary

In the *Times,* scanning the photo,
Narrow column-wide, of George as
He had looked in nineteen thirty-
Four. And that was all of that.

And for the unproselytizing
Sect of the Rememberers—
I, the boy then, some of you—
All our various vaudevilles are
Giving way to faster brighter
Dumber slower stuff, and even
Stories told of them perform their
Dimming time-steps as they slowly
Shuffle off to Buffalo. And
Not to speak of George Moran, for
(This the boy remembered) as the
"Early Bird" skit ended, *Well, who
Cares about worms, anyhow?*

BEACH WHISPERS

In the night wind astir
The pale dune grasses sing
"We are what we always whirr,
Food for ruminant thought,"
Soft, neither out of tune
Nor in it as their commotion
Mingles with the hiss
Of water falling all over
Itself to claim the sand.
Ears open and eyes shut
We barely understand
What they could be said to say
About the neap and spring
Of tides and even more
About how to uncover
The orders of all this:
The crown of the bright moon,
The fiefdom of the ocean,
The serfdom of the shore,
(Such dark politics) and,
Nightly feigning his role
Of deus absconditus, sole
Absentee landlord of all,
Some otherwhere the sun
Reigns from his distant hall.

NOTES

A FRAGMENT TWICE REPAIRED   J. M. Edmonds edited the text of Sappho for the Loeb edition; Oxyrynchus: the place in upper Egypt where so many ancient literary papyri were found.

FORGET HOW TO REMEMBER HOW TO FORGET   Phaedrus: Socrates suggested to him that the invention of writing led to the weakening of the human faculty of memory.

GETTING FROM HERE TO THERE   Stephen Yenser reminded me of this word-game of Lewis Carroll's, in which you move from one word to an unrelated one through a series of one-letter substitutions. There seemed to be a parable here.

ACROSS THE BOARD   "Come back home wid a pocket full ob tin": Stephen Foster, "The Camptown Races"; *vaut le voyage:* high praise for a restaurant in the Michelin guide.

X'S SYNDROME   Tapanuli Fever and The Black Formosa Corruption are notional diseases propounded by Sherlock Holmes; Madura Foot is quite actual.

FIRE!   Gaston Bachelard's book is called in English *The Psychoanalysis of Fire.*

DIGITAL   Bocca della Verità a grotesque face in low relief on the outer wall of Santa Maria in Cosmedin in Rome, into whose mouth only truth-tellers may put their hands with impunity.

OWL   Queen of the Air: Minerva chose the owl as her companion because its predecessor, the crow, talked too much. Helmsman of life: *"Philosophia Biou Kubernêtês"* is the motto of the Phi Beta Kappa Society. Wagon: the Wain, the Big Dipper, pointing toward Polaris and guiding fugitive slaves northward (and hence "Swing Low, Sweet Chariot"?)

FIGUREHEAD   dolphin-striker: a spar used for mooring.

M AND M'S   *"Eheu . . . fugaces labuntur anni"* ("Oy, how quickly the years pass!") condensed from Horace, *Odes* II.14.

EMBLEM   Each page of a 16th-17th-century emblem book displayed a woodcut or engraving with some moralizing and allegorizing verses below it. This is an emblem-shaped poem.

TWO GLOSSES ON RENÉ MAGRITTE   "Private Parts" refers to *L'Évidence éternelle (The Eternally Obvious),* 1930, oil on five separately framed canvases showing respectively a female face, breasts, belly, knees and feet, hung vertically in order. "Painted Nude" invokes *The Attempt of the Impossible,* 1928, which shows an artist in a room, painting not on a canvas, but in thin air, the left arm of an otherwise completed nude female figure standing before him, three-dimensional, in the room.

SUN IN AN EMPTY ROOM   *In lumine tuo videbimus lumen* (Ps.36.9) and its translation, "in thy radiance we see light": the motto on the seal, and a line from the alma mater, of Columbia University, where I was schooled.

ERASING A BAD NAME   The last line invokes Wittgenstein, *Tractatus,* Preface, and final proposition: "Whereof one cannot speak thereof one must be silent."

CHARLES SHEELER'S THE ARTIST LOOKS AT NATURE   Nature and painting: *Pope, An Essay on Criticism* I 185: "Nature and Homer were, he found, the same."

GHAZAL   "Less than the dust . . . weed . . . rust . . . etc." and "Take here thy sword, I make it keen and bright; Love's last reward, death comes for me tonight" etc. are from "Less than the dust" Laurence Hope (Mrs. M. H. Nicolson, 1865–1904) who wrote volumes of verse such as *The Garden of Kama and Other Love Lyrics from India,* of which "Pale Hands I Loved" used to be the best known.

EARLY BIRDS   Oakland: Gertrude Stein is said to have remarked about that city, "There's no there there."

A NOTE ABOUT THE AUTHOR

John Hollander's first book of poems, *A Crackling of Thorns,*
was chosen by W. H. Auden as the 1958 volume in the Yale
Series of Younger Poets. Since then he has published sixteen
additional books of poems including this one. (A list appears at
the beginning of this volume). He is the author of eight critical
works, the most recent *The Poetry of Everyday Life* (1998), and
a number of anthologies, among them *Poems of Our Moment*
and *Committed to Memory: 100 Best Poems to Memorize.* He was
a co-editor of *The Oxford Anthology of English Literature* and a
co-editor (with Anthony Hecht, with whom he shared the
Bollingen Prize in Poetry in 1983) of *Jiggery-Pokery: A Com-
pendium of Double Dactyls.* He attended Columbia and Indi-
ana Universities, was a junior fellow of the Society of Fellows
at Harvard University, taught at Connecticut College and
Yale, and was Professor of English at Hunter College and the
Graduate Center, CUNY. He is currently Sterling Professor
of English at Yale. In 1990 he was made a Fellow of the
MacArthur Foundation.

A NOTE ON THE TYPE

This book was set in Granjon, a type named in compliment to
Robert Granjon but neither a copy of a classic face nor an
entirely original creation. George W. Jones based his designs
on the type used by Claude Garamond (c. 1480–1561) in his
beautiful French books. Granjon more closely resembles
Garamond's own type than does any of the various modern
types that bear his name.

Robert Granjon began his career as type cutter in 1523. The
boldest and most original designer of his time, he was one of
the first to practice the trade of type founder apart from that of
printer. Between 1557 and 1562 Granjon printed about twenty
books in types designed by himself, following, after the fash-
ion, the cursive handwriting of the time. These types, usually
known as *caractères de civilité,* he himself called *lettres fran-
çaises,* as especially appropriate to his own country.

Composition by NK Graphics, Keene, New Hampshire
Printed at The Stinehour Press, Lunenburg, Vermont
Bound by Quebecor Vermont, Brattleboro, Vermont
Designed by Harry Ford